FROM THE CRESCENT TO THE CROSS

MARK HAYATE ABADI

The story of a former Imam
and his road to salvation and healing.

An amazing testimony of God's Love
and Saving Power

© 2021 by *Hayate Abadi Ministries*
ISBN: 978-0-9828843-9-3

All rights reserved. This book is protected by the copyright laws of the United States of America. This book may not be copied or reprinted for commercial gain or profit. The use of quotations or photocopying for personal or group study, or for free distribution without distorting the original work, is permitted and encouraged. Credit and contact information must be included as follows: "From The Crescent To The Cross" www.hayateabadi.org. Copyright © 2021 by *Hayate Abadi Ministries*. Used by permission." Other permission may be granted upon request.

Scripture quotations are taken from the following Bible versions:
The New King James Version. Copyright © 1982 by Thomas Nelson, Inc. Used by permission. All rights reserved.
The NEW AMERICAN STANDARD BIBLE®, Copyright © 1960,1962,1963,1968,1971,1972,1973,1975,1977, 1995 by The Lockman Foundation. Used by permission.
The HOLY BIBLE, NEW INTERNATIONAL VERSION®. Copyright © 1973, 1978, 1984 Biblica. Used by permission of Zondervan. All rights reserved.

Abbreviations are as follows:
NKJV – New King James Version
NASB – New American Standard Bible
NIV – New International Version

Edited by Dr. Haakon Smith

Blue Diamond Bookhouse
www.bluediamondbookhouse.com

www.hayateabadi.org

My name is Mark. I was raised in a very religious Muslim family in Southern Iran. I was a student of the Quran from an early age. My father built a mosque. At the age of 6 he brought me to the mosque and asked the local Imam to train me in the tenets of Islam. Although I prayed, fasted, and observed the religious laws, I was always plagued with the question of where I would spend eternity. When I asked the leader of the mosque, He would tell me, "Just do what I say, and do not ask questions." Yet, no matter what I did, I still lacked the assurance that I would go to heaven when I died. I knew in my heart that I could not do what it would take to please a holy God.

At the age of six I saw a girl who also was six years old. I felt love in my heart for her, and I knew that she would become my future wife. I wrote a lovely letter to her. Naturally, she could not read it, so she passed it on to her dad and they started laughing. I waited for 12 years, and finally we got married. A few years later our son was born and he was a lovely boy. Then I went to Mecca with my parents. While I was praying there, a man tapped me on my shoulder and told me that Allah wanted me to divorce my wife because I had not prayed with a pronunciation that was 100% correct in Arabic.

I felt that something was not right with this message. I said to him that if Allah knew that I lived in Iran speaking the Farsi language, he would be able to understand me when I prayed to him. Otherwise, he would not be the true, living God. I decided to leave Mecca early and return to Iran.

Sometime later as I was driving in the snow with my family, I lost control of the car. It flipped over eight times. Fortunately, my family members were OK. However, I sustained severe nerve damage in my left leg. The injury was so bad that I was confined to crutches and a wheelchair, paralyzed with pain. My wife had to go to work, and she became my caregiver. People accused me of being cursed by Allah for leaving Mecca. Although I had back surgeries twice, the doctors in Iran could not find any cure for my condition.

After 14 years in my weak and terrible condition, I decided to go to London to seek medical help. In London, I went to four different surgeons and got four different opinions. I cried out, "I think this is the end; God where are you?" My thoughts turned to suicide as I thought I had become a burden to my wife and kids.

That night I fell asleep before my wife did and I had a dream. Twice I heard a voice say, "Go to the United States." I woke my wife up and she thought that I needed help to change my position in bed as she used to help me several times during the night because I could not turn around on my own. I let her know that I did not need her help with that. I shared my dream with her and she encouraged me to go back to sleep. She said that I had eaten too much pizza.

My dream soon became a reality as God opened the door for us to travel to the United States. In a matter of few days, we obtained a Visa. We went to Washington State, to the home of my relative. He took me to an orthopedic surgeon who ran a series of tests. After a couple of days, the doctor told me that he could do nothing!

A few days later I received a call from the doctor who told me that he was going to perform surgery on my back. With expenses up to 25,000 dollars, I did not have such an amount of money to pay. There could also be a 99% chance that I would lose the nerve that goes from my back to the left leg.

My relative allowed me and my wife to stay in his home rent free while he traveled to Iran to get married. Before he left, he introduced me to his neighbor. I called him and asked if he could take me to another good doctor who would not be expensive. After seeing how weak I was and hearing the story of my pain, they promised to take me to a doctor.

Praise God for His awesome plan! The neighbors were Christians and their parents had been missionaries to Iran! A few days later, they said, "let us go", and they carried me to their car. While they were driving, the neighbor asked me, "I know you are Muslim. What do you believe about Jesus Christ?" I said: "Stop, are you taking me to the doctor? So why do you need to ask me who Jesus Christ is? What is the correlation between Jesus Christ and my sickness?" He said, "I just want to know your opinion." I said, "He was one of the prophets and he died like all the prophets." My neighbor said that he wanted to tell me the rest of the story. After Jesus died, He rose from the dead on the third day and He is alive now. He is the Son of God. I said, "What, you make a man

God?!" He said, "I don't make a man God. He himself proclaimed to be God. God became man so that man could become a child of God."

When we arrived in Puyallup, a suburb just south of Seattle, there was no hospital or clinic there. Instead, we arrived at what is called a passion play. It was an outdoor drama that reenacted the Life, death, and resurrection of Jesus. My neighbor said, "My doctor is Jesus Christ." I was initially reluctant and did not want to go to the play. I thought that Jesus was not my prophet, He is their prophet, and I do not want to listen to that program. I was searching for an excuse not to go to the performance. In my condition, I could not sit for hours. The neighbor was quite thoughtful, however, so he paid for more seats so that I could lie down. I finally gave in.

What I experienced that evening I will never forget. The one, the only one who had never sinned, who had no sin, became sin for me and took my sin upon himself. My eyes were opened that night and my heart was touched. I realized that what the Bible says is true. God is love. Not that God has love, but He *is* love. When they showed that He rose again from the dead I knew that He is God and my heart was changed.

The next week, the neighbor invited me and my wife to church. A woman there who greeted us noticed my Farsi accent and she asked me where I was from? I was amazed. In Mecca I was rejected by Allah because of my accent, and I was informed of the penalty that I was required to divorce my wife. I was shocked; I had been wondering if people in the church would similarly impose a penalty on me because of my Farsi accent. But she let me know that she could tell that I was from Iran and that there were Iranian Christians who had been former Muslims. I also found that there is a Bible in the Farsi language. When a group of Christians gathered around me and offered to pray for me because of my infirmity, I told them that for most of my life, I had prayed in the mosque, but that I had not received any healing. They told me that there would be a difference as they were going to pray for me in the name of Jesus. The Lord told his followers to pray in His name and they would receive whatever they asked for when they believed. In Matthew 21:22 it is written: "^{22} And whatever things you ask in prayer, believing, you will receive" **(Matthew 21:22 NKJV)**.

A week later, the pastor and the elders of the church came to my home and shared the gospel with us. When they invited us to come to their fellowship and learn more about the word of God, I said "Sir, I have a question." Knowing that I was a Muslim, the pastor was expecting a difficult question about the trinity. Instead, I asked: "how do I give my life to Jesus Christ?" I explained that I had already found the answer to my questions when I understood that Jesus died on the cross for me.

That night, I saw my wife crying out. I asked: What has happened to you?" She answered: "The same thing that happened to you. I believe in Christ as my Lord and Savior, too." That evening marked a turning point in my life. Whenever I remember that evening I say: "Lord, thank you. Thank you that you brought me out of the darkness and brought me into your marvelous light." That evening the gates of heaven were opened to me. Not because I was a good person. Not because I was searching for Him. Not because I was trying to reach Him, but because he reached out to me.

My wife and I went to the fellowship every week to listen to the word of God and grow in our faith. After about two months, in the middle of the night I woke up with feeling in my left leg. My wife took me to the hospital and my doctor examined me and asked me who had done such a great surgery? I answered: "You are my doctor and I praise God for your talent, but my condition was so bad that nobody except one could do it." My doctor asked me the name of the surgeon that did the surgery on my back, and I told him that His name is Jesus!

My doctor asked me if I was excited, and I said no. I told him that I was excited because I got saved. "I can die of a heart attack in your office because of the joy that I have now, but I know for sure that I'll see my Lord."

I praise God for his healing power. But the reason for my real excitement is the joy of salvation that the Lord has given to me. I now know that at the end of my life, whenever that may be, Jesus will be standing there to receive me. That is the answer to the question that haunted me from my youth. I had found it in Christ, eternal life in Him, because of Him. He also wants to be Lord and Savior in your life, but you need to let Jesus come into your heart today.

After I got saved the Lord filled me with The Holy Spirit, and a few months later my wife and I attended a Christian Iranian camp meeting. When one of the pastors laid hands on me and prayed for me, I was touched by The Holy Spirit. I had a vision and saw Jesus coming and I was trying to hang onto his feet. I asked him take me home to be with him. He said: "Not now, I have something for you to do."

In the middle of the night The Holy Spirit sent me to a small chapel on the campgrounds and he guided me to read Psalm 51, when I had read that Psalm, I discovered what the Lord wanted me to do in verse 13:

Then **I will teach transgressors Your ways,
and sinners will be converted to You.**

Psalm 51:
Be gracious to me, O God, according to Your lovingkindness;
According to the greatness of Your compassion blot out my transgressions.
^{2} Wash me thoroughly from my iniquity
And cleanse me from my sin.
^{3} For I know my transgressions,
And my sin is ever before me.
^{4} Against You, You only, I have sinned
And done what is evil in Your sight,
So that You are justified when You speak
And blameless when You judge.
^{5} Behold, I was brought forth in iniquity,
And in sin my mother conceived me.
^{6} Behold, You desire truth in the innermost being,
And in the hidden part You will make me know wisdom.
^{7} Purify me with hyssop, and I shall be clean; wash me, and I shall be whiter than snow.
^{8} Make me to hear joy and gladness,
Let the bones which You have broken rejoice.
^{9} Hide Your face from my sins
And blot out all my iniquities.
^{10} Create in me a clean heart, O God,
And renew a steadfast spirit within me.
^{11} Do not cast me away from Your presence
And do not take Your The Holy Spirit from me.

[12] Restore to me the joy of Your salvation
And sustain me with a willing spirit.
[13] *Then* I will teach transgressors Your ways,
And sinners will be converted to You.
[14] Deliver me from bloodguiltiness, O God, the God of my salvation;
Then my tongue will joyfully sing of Your righteousness.
[15] O Lord, open my lips,
That my mouth may declare Your praise.
[16] For You do not delight in sacrifice, otherwise I would give it;
You are not pleased with burnt offering.
[17] The sacrifices of God are a broken spirit;
A broken and a contrite heart, O God, You will not despise.
[18] By Your favor do good to Zion;
Build the walls of Jerusalem.
[19] Then You will delight in righteous sacrifices,
In burnt offering and whole burnt offering;
Then young bulls will be offered on Your altar. **(Psalm 51 NASB)**

The Lord wanted me to share his love and truth with people, so I started to read the Bible, and I attended a seminary to learn more about Jesus so that I would be better equipped to share him with others.

I also attended evangelist classes at the Church. There I had two teachers who gave me motivation and encouragement. They tried to help me become a disciple of Jesus. Their names were Gary Weiner and John Gunderson. John asked me to take over His position who was the head trainer. Praise God for both of them.

My pastor, Yusef Nazir, was a great man of God and when he preached a sermon, he always gave an altar call. People were encouraged to repent of their sins, invite Jesus into their hearts, and to make him their only Lord and Savior. When you make such a commitment to God, you can have a personal relationship with Him, just as I and other Christians do. The Bible confirms this as well in John 14:23. Jesus replied, "Anyone who loves me will obey my teaching. My Father will love them, and we will come to them and make our home with them." **(John 14:23 NIV)**

WHO IS GOD TO YOU?

He is my HEALER (Psalm 103:3)
He is my REDEEMER (Isaiah 59:20)
He is my DELIVERER (Psalm 70:5)
He is my STRENGTH (Psalm 43:2)
He is my SHELTER (Joel 3:16)
He is my FRIEND (John 15:15)
He is my ADVOCATE (1 John 2:1)
He is my RESTORER (Psalm 23:3)
He is my EVERLASTING FATHER (Isaiah 9:6)
He is LOVE (1 John 4:16)
He is my MEDIATOR (1 Timothy 2:5-6)
He is my STRONGHOLD (Nahum 1:7)
He is the BREAD OF LIFE (John 6:35)
He is my HIDING PLACE (Psalm 32:7)
He is the EVERLASTING LIGHT (Isaiah 60:20)
He is a STRONG TOWER (Proverbs 18:10)
He is my RESTING PLACE (Jeremiah 50:6)
He is the SPIRIT OF TRUTH (John 16:13)
He is my REFUGE FROM THE STORM (Isaiah 25:4)
He is ETERNAL LIFE (1 John 5:20)
He is the LORD WHO PROVIDES (Genesis 22:14)
He is the LORD OF PEACE (2 Thessalonians 3:16)
He is the LIVING WATER (John 4:10)
He is my SHIELD (Psalm 144:2)
He is my HUSBAND (Isaiah 54:5)
He is my HELPER (Hebrews 13:6)
He is my WONDERFUL COUNSELOR (Isaiah 9:6)
He is the LORD WHO HEALS (Exodus 15:26)

The Final Judge

In Joel chapter 3, Yahweh declares that the nations will be gathered in the valley of Jehoshaphat and that he will enter into judgment with them there on behalf of his people and inheritance, Israel, because they were scattered among the nations. They also have divided up the land, among other reasons mentioned in verse 3. **(Joel 3:2)** Thus, in verse 12 we can read: "Let the nations be aroused and come up to the valley of Jehoshaphat, for there I will sit to judge all the surrounding nations." **(Joel 3:12)** According to the prophet David, "the Lord abides forever; He has established His throne for judgment, and He will judge the world in righteousness." **(Psalm 9:7)**

The Quran maintains that Allah will judge the world, rewarding believers and punishing unbelievers:

Quran 22:56-57 The kingdom on that day shall be Allah's; He will judge between them; so those who believe and do good will be in gardens of bliss. And (as for) those who disbelieve in and reject our communications, these it is who shall have a disgraceful chastisement.

So why, we may wonder, would Jesus tell his followers that he will be the final judge of all people?

Matthew 25:31-32: But when the Son of Man comes in His glory, and all the angles with Him, then He will sit on His glorious throne, All the nations will be gathered before Him, and He will separate them one from another, as a shepherd divides his sheep from the goats. And He will set the sheep on His right hand, but the goats on the left. Then the King will say to those on His right hand, 'Come, you blessed of My Father, inherit the Kingdom prepared for you from the foundation of the world.'

The Light

In **Psalm 27:1**, David proclaims: The Lord is my light and my salvation.

John 8:12: "I am the Light of the world; he who follows Me will not walk in the darkness, but will have the Light of life."

The Truth

David refers to Yahweh as the "God of Truth" (Psalm 31:5).

John 14:6: Jesus said to him, "I am the way, and the truth, and the life; no one comes to the Father but through Me."

Resurrection

1 Samuel 2:6: "The Lord kills and makes alive; He brings down to Sheol and raises up."

John 5:25-29: ^{25} Truly, truly, I say to you, an hour is coming and now is, when the dead will hear the voice of the Son of God, and those who hear will live. ^{26} For just as the Father has life in Himself, even so He gave to the Son also to have life in Himself; ^{27} and He gave Him authority to execute judgment, because He is *the* Son of Man. ^{28} Do not marvel at this; for an hour is coming, in which all who are in the tombs will hear His voice, ^{29} and will come forth; those who did the good *deeds* to a resurrection of life, those who committed the evil *deeds* to a resurrection of judgment.

John 5:21-23: ^{21} For just as the Father raises the dead and gives them life, even so the Son also gives life to whom He wishes. ^{22} For not even the Father judges anyone, but He has given all judgment to the Son, ^{23} so that all will honor the Son even as they honor the Father. He who does not honor the Son does not honor the Father who sent Him.

John 11:25: Jesus said to her, "I am the resurrection and the life; he who believes in Me will live even if he dies."

God's Glory

Isaiah 42:5: "I am the Lord, that is My name; I will not give My glory to another,

John 17:5: Now, Father, glorify Me together with Yourself, with the glory which I had with You before the world was.

Matthew 22:41-45: Now while the Pharisees were gathered together, Jesus asked them a question: ^{42} "What do you think about the Christ, whose son is He?" They said to Him, "*The son* of David." He said to them, "Then how does David in the Spirit call Him 'Lord,' saying, ^{44} 'The Lord said to my Lord, "Sit at My right hand, Until I put Your enemies beneath Your feet'"? [45] If David then calls Him 'Lord,' how is He his son?" [46] No one was able to answer Him a word, nor did anyone dare from that day on to ask Him another question.

God Uses Cyrus

Isaiah 45:1-7:
1 "Thus says the LORD to His anointed, To Cyrus, whose right hand I have held--To subdue nations before him And loose the armor of kings, To open before him the double doors, So that the gates will not be shut: 2 'I will go before you And make the crooked places straight; I will break in pieces the gates of bronze And cut the bars of iron. 3 I will give you the treasures of darkness And hidden riches of secret places, That you may know that I, the LORD, Who call [you] by your name, [Am] the God of Israel. 4 For Jacob My servant's sake, And Israel My elect, I have even called you by your name; I have named you, though you have not known Me. 5 I [am] the LORD, and [there is] no other; [There is] no God besides Me. I will gird you, though you have not known Me, 6 That they may know from the rising of the sun to its setting That [there is] none besides Me. I [am] the LORD, and [there is] no other; 7 I form the light and create darkness, I make peace and create calamity; I, the LORD, do all these [things].'

Psalm 83:1-4:
1 A Song. A Psalm of Asaph. Do not keep silent, O God! Do not hold Your peace, And do not be still, O God! 2 For behold, Your enemies make a tumult; And those who hate You have lifted up their head. 3 They have taken crafty counsel against Your people, And consulted together against Your sheltered ones. 4 They have said, "Come, and let us cut them off from [being] a nation, That the name of Israel may be remembered no more."

Persian people compare what we had—Cyrus who was anointed by the Lord—with the Islamic Republic of Iran's goal to destroy Israel. Wow, it is exactly what Psalm 83:1-4 says.

In Quran chapter 5 verse 72-73:
They do blaspheme who say: "God is Christ the son of Mary." But said Christ: "O children of Israel! worship God my Lord and your Lord." Whoever joins other gods with God will forbid him the garden and the

Fire will be his abode. There will for the wrong-doers be no one to help.

T73:
They do blaspheme who say: God is one of three in a Trinity: for there is no god except One God. If they desist not from their word (of blasphemy) verily a grievous penalty will befall the blasphemers among them.

Could you tell me if you think that Islam is a religion of peace? Then consider what is written in the Quran:

Quran chapter 2:191:
And slay them wherever ye catch them and turn them out from where they have turned you out; for tumult and oppression are worse than slaughter; but fight them not at the Sacred Mosque unless they (first) fight you there; but if they fight you slay them. Such is the reward of those who suppress faith.

Quran chapter 3:28:
Let not the believers take for friends or helpers unbelievers rather than believers; if any do that in nothing will there be help from God; except by way of precaution that ye may guard yourselves from them. But God cautions you (to remember) Himself for the final goals to God.

Quran chapter 3:85
If anyone desires a religion other than Islam (submission to God) never will it be accepted of him; and in the Hereafter, he will be in the ranks of those who have lost (all spiritual good).

Quran chapter 5:33:
The punishment of those who wage war against God and His Apostle and strive with might and main for mischief through the land is: execution or crucifixion of the cutting off of hands and feet from opposite sides or exile from the land: that is their disgrace in this world and a heavy punishment is theirs in the Hereafter.

Quran chapter 8:12:
Remember thy Lord inspired the angels (with the message): "I am with you: give firmness to the believers: I will instill terror into the hearts of

the unbelievers: smite ye above their necks and smite all their fingertips off them."

Quran chapter 8:60:
Against them make ready your strength to the utmost of your power including steeds of war to strike terror into (the hearts of) the enemies of God and your enemies and others besides whom ye may not know but whom God doth know. Whatever ye shall spend in the cause of God shall be repaid unto you and ye shall not be treated unjustly.

Quran chapter 8:65:
Apostle! rouse the believers to the fight. If there are twenty amongst you patient and persevering they will vanquish two hundred: if a hundred they will vanquish a thousand of the unbelievers: for these are a people without understanding.

Quran chapter 9:5:
But when the forbidden months are past then fight and slay the pagans wherever ye find them and seize them beleaguer them and lie in wait for them in every stratagem (of war); but if they repent and establish regular prayers and practice regular charity then open the way for them: for God is Oft-Forgiving Most Merciful.

Quran chapter 9:30:
The Jews call Uzair a son of God and the Christians call Christ the son of God. That is a saying from their mouths; (in this) they but imitate what the unbelievers of old used to say. God's curse be on them: how they are deluded away from the truth!

Quran chapter 9:123:
O ye who believe! fight the unbelievers who gird you about and let them find firmness in you; and know that God is with those who fear him.

Quran chapter 22:19:
These two antagonists dispute With each other about their Lord : But those who deny (their Lord),— For them will be cut out A garment of Fire : Over their heads will be Poured out boiling water.

Quran chapter 47:4:
Therefore, when ye meet The Unbelievers (in fight), Smite at their necks; At length, when ye have Thoroughly subdued them, Bind a bond Firmly (on them) : thereafter (Is the time for) either Generosity or ransom : Until the war lays down Its burdens. Thus (are ye Commanded) : but if it Had been God's Will, He could certainly have exacted Retribution from them (Himself) ; but (He lets you fight) In order to test you, Some with others. But those who are slain In the way of God,—He will never let Their deeds be lost.

Islam Denies the Trinity

Quran chapter 4:171:
O people of the Book! commit no excesses in your religion: nor say of God aught but truth. Christ Jesus the son of Mary was (no more than) an Apostle of God and His Word which He bestowed on Mary and a Spirit proceeding from Him: so believe in God and His Apostles. Say not "Trinity": desist: it will be better for you: for God is One God: glory be to him: (for Exalted is He) above having a son. To Him belong all things in the heavens and on earth. And enough is God as a Disposer of affairs.

Islam Denies the Crucifixion

Quran chapter 4:157:
That they said (in boast) "We killed Christ Jesus the son of Mary the Apostle of God"; but they killed him not nor crucified him but so it was made to appear to them and those who differ therein are full of doubts with no (certain) knowledge but only conjecture to follow for of a surety they killed him not.

Islam Denies the Resurrection

If Islam rejected the crucifixion, then there would be no resurrection. But in John 11:25-26 we see the resurrection: [25]Jesus said to her, "I am the resurrection and the life; he who believes In Me will live even If he dies, [26]and everyone who lives and believes in Me will never die. Do you believe this?" **(John 11:25-26)**

Quran chapter 3 verse 54 – Allah is the greatest deceiver

Would you please compare Jesus, the son of God with Allah?

The Bible says in John 3:16: "For God so loved the world, that He gave His only begotten Son, that whoever believes in Him shall not perish, but have eternal life. **(John 3:16)**

You now have a choice; do you still want to follow Islam, or are you ready to invite Jesus into your heart as your Lord and Savior. One day I shared the Gospel with some people and The Holy Spirit changed their hearts. These are some testimonies that came forth after that meeting.

Being Filled with the Power of The Holy Spirit

In Acts 1:8 we can read: "But you will receive power when The Holy Spirit has come upon you." After I got saved, I was afraid of sharing the gospel with people, even my friend Hussein whom I used to live with before I knew the Lord. I remember that Hussein once asked me why I was dressed so nicely and if I was going to church. I said no because I was afraid of telling him that I was a Christian. Consequently, I felt bad that I did not tell him the truth.

A few months later, I attended a Christian conference and I was crying and asking the Lord to please fill me with The Holy Spirit. When the pastor placed his hand upon me, I suddenly felt the overwhelming presence of the Lord. I was hanging onto his feet the entire time and asking the Lord to take me home, but he told me that the time had not yet come. For hours nobody could talk to me because I was rejoicing in the presence of the Lord. They carried me to my bed, and I fell asleep. I was awakened and I remembered that in the middle of the night The Holy Spirit told me to get up and read Psalm 51.

I went to a small chapel near the conference location, and I read Psalm 51.

In Psalm 51 it is written: 1 For the music director. A Psalm of David, when Nathan the prophet came to him, after he had gone in to Bathsheba. Be gracious to me, God, according to Your faithfulness; According to the greatness of Your compassion, wipe out my wrongdoings. 2 Wash me thoroughly from my guilt and cleanse me from my sin. 3 For I know my wrongdoings, and my sin is constantly before me. 4 Against You, You only, I have sinned and done what is evil in Your sight, so that You are justified when You speak and blameless when You judge. 5 Behold, I was brought forth in guilt, and in sin my mother conceived me. 6 Behold, You desire truth in the innermost being, and in secret You will make wisdom known to me. 7 Purify me with hyssop, and I will be clean; cleanse me, and I will be whiter than snow. 8 Let me hear joy and gladness, let the bones You have broken rejoice. 9 Hide Your face from my sins and wipe out all my guilty deeds. 10 Create in me a clean heart, God, and renew a steadfast spirit within me. 11 Do not cast me away from Your presence, and do not take Your Holy Spirit from me. 12 Restore to me the joy of Your salvation, and sustain me with a willing spirit. 13 [Then] I will teach wrongdoers Your ways, and sinners will be converted to You. 14 Save me from the guilt of bloodshed, God, the God of my salvation; [then] my tongue will joyfully sing of Your righteousness. 15 Lord, open my lips, so that my mouth may declare Your praise. 16 For You do not delight in sacrifice, otherwise I would give it; You do not take pleasure in burnt offering. 17 The sacrifices of God are a broken spirit; a broken and a contrite heart, God, You will not despise. 18 By Your favor do good to Zion; build the walls of Jerusalem. 19 Then You will delight in righteous sacrifices, in burnt offering and whole burnt offering; then bulls will be offered on Your altar. **(Psalm 51:1-19 NASB)**

When I read that Psalm it touched my heart and I knew that the Lord had called me to share his good news. As soon as I returned from the retreat I visited my friend Hussein and shared with him that I was ashamed to tell him that I am a Christian and that I attend church.

I told him to sit down and that I wanted to share the gospel with him. He was not pleased with my declaration and he rejected me and told me that he did not want to see me anymore.

A few months later, I attended a class on how to share the gospel. The first night of the class the pastor asked me: "What are you doing here?" I told him the Lord had called me to share the good news and I would like to be trained in the word of God. At the end of the first class-session a young man came to me and he said: "You are an answer to my prayer." He knew an Iranian family (a mother named N and her four children). They did not speak English, and he wanted to share the gospel with them. Since they could not communicate with me in English, he was excited that I was speaking Farsi and consequently, I could converse with them and share the gospel. He gave me their phone number and I called N and I invited her with the kids to our church.

On the way to church, I was talking to her and the children, sharing the story in the Bible where Abraham was told by God to sacrifice his son Isaac. The Quran states that Abraham wanted to sacrifice his son Ishmael (Arabic: Ismail). We arrived at the church and the pastor was sharing a sermon on the same subject that we discussed on the way to church. N was so amazed. She knew that this message was from the Lord because both the pastor and I had spoken about the same subject, and she was with me the whole time.

N's husband died of cancer years before, and she had three sons and one daughter. Her eldest son, Al, was so depressed because of his father's death, and he did not want to talk to anybody, even his mother. He would go to school but not attend classes.

When the Lord brought this family into our lives, I started sharing the Gospel and also showing them the love of the Lord, especially the older son. Several weeks later, one night, my pastor and I went to their home and asked them if they were ready to invite Christ into their hearts. The mother pleaded with us not to ask her older son. She said that he did not speak, and because of that I was feeling bad for him. But then I started to ask that son if he had heard the gospel in the last few weeks and if he understood what we were sharing. I asked him to open his heart to the Lord and suddenly Al said: "Yes, I would like to invite Christ into my heart as my Lord and Savior." Everybody was crying, especially his mother, because he had not spoken for two years. And now he could suddenly speak.

After a few weeks they were ready to get baptized and N invited her sister and her brother-in-law to participate at the baptism. Her brother-in-law was mad at me because we were having a baptism. He asked me when someone was immersed into water how that would make them clean and their sins would be forgiven. He was blaming me and said that he was the reason they used to believe in Allah. How could I then turn them away from Islam? I told them that only God can change people, not I. After the baptism I invited them and her brother-in-law's family to come to our home for dinner the following Saturday.

They came to our apartment and we had dinner together. After dinner the conversation started, and her brother-in-law began debating, in his quest to convert me back to Islam. He asked me many questions, and I did not have all the answers since I was a babe in Christ. So anytime that I did not know the answers I would call my pastor, and I received answers from him that enabled me to share the gospel with them more accurately. Dinner and conversation started at 6 PM and ended at 3 AM and when they left, her brother-in-law told me that he was going to read the Quran, and he would come back and convert me to Islam. I let him know that he should not waste his time; Christ promised me that he is not going to forsake me.

We said our goodbyes. A couple of days later when I came home (Monday evening), my wife was having a conversation on the phone that she seemed to be enjoying. She asked me to guess who it was that had called her. It turned out to be the brother-in-law of N, the person who wanted to convert me to Islam. He said that they all could not fall asleep when they came home from the dinner party. They had invited Christ into their hearts. My pastor taught basic principles of Christianity in several sessions and then they were all baptized, N's brother-in-law, sister, nephew, and niece all got baptized. Yes, there is a power in the word of God. Yes, The Holy Spirit can convince people, and the Bible says the Truth shall set them free. (John 8:32)

Because the Muslims do not know the truth, they love to argue with you and they maintain that the Bible has been corrupted. If you ask them if they have read the Quran, many actually do not know its content. The Quran is in Arabic and the Iranian language is Farsi, so consequently, they do not know it. I therefore encourage you to make a strong suggestion to Muslims that they need to read the Quran and compare it with the Bible, and they will be able to find the truth in the Bible. Always focus on the word of God, not on the word of the Quran, because there is a power in the word of God. Praise the Lord! N's family are all now believers in God. N's brother-in-law and her sister are now pastors in an Iranian speaking church.

We give all the glory and honor to Him who will call His people. I am not ashamed of the Gospel, because it is the power of God for salvation of everyone who believes; first Jew, then for the Gentile. If you hear the voice of the Lord calling you, do not reject Him because the Bible says that every knee shall bow down and every tongue shall confess that He is Lord **(Philippians 2:10)**. It is better to believe in Him and receive Him as Lord and Savior. Make a decision to receive Him today, because we do not know how long we may live and what could happen to us in the next minutes of our lives.

John 3:16 says:
For God so loved the world that he gave his one and only Son, so that whoever believes in him shall not perish but have eternal life.

Ephesians 2:8-10:
8 For by grace you have been saved through faith, and that not of yourselves; it is the gift of God, 9 not of works, lest anyone should boast. 10 For we are His workmanship, created in Christ Jesus.

Matthew 28:19-20:
19 Go therefore and make disciples of all the nations, baptizing them in the name of the Father and of the Son and of The Holy Spirit, 20 teaching them to observe all things that I have commanded you; and lo, I am with you always, even to the end of the age." Amen.

Are you ready? The Lord is always ready to accept you. He loves you.

The Power of Worship

The Holy Spirit has empowered me to share the Gospel with people.

When I got the calling from God to preach God's word through Satellite TV, I was obedient to the Lord. I started sharing the word of God from the book of Ester. I shared how its content is relevant for the time we live in today. As the banner for our ministry broadcast we use the worship song "Open the eyes of my heart, I want to see Jesus."

Six hours after the first broadcast, a young man from Shiraz in Iran called me and told me that he was 33 years old with a Master's degree in Computer Science. He was very healthy and wealthy and had a wonderful wife. She also earned a Master's degree, but he was not content and happy with that, and he became so upset that he attempted suicide. Waiting for his wife to fall asleep, he took some sleeping pills to end his life.

His TV was on, and at the same time that our program started to broadcast, he heard the song, "Open the eyes of my heart." This worship song captured and touched his heart, and he said that he would wait until the end of the song to commit suicide. After the song I started to share the gospel and he said that he would "wait to see what this old man had to say." I was sharing that when God created Adam and Eve, he even gave him the privilege to name the animals.

Genesis 2:8-9:
[8] The Lord God planted a garden toward the east, in Eden; and there He placed the man whom He had formed. [9] Out of the ground the Lord God caused to grow every tree that is pleasing to the sight and good for food; the tree of life also in the midst of the garden, and the tree of the knowledge of good and evil.

Genesis 2:15-25:
[15] Then the Lord God took the man and put him into the Garden of Eden to cultivate it and keep it. [16] The Lord God commanded the man, saying, "From any tree of the garden you may eat freely; [17] but from the tree of the knowledge of good and evil you shall not eat, for in the day that you eat from it you will surely die." [18] Then the Lord God said, "It is not good for the man to be alone; I will make him a helper suitable for him." [19] Out of the ground the Lord God formed every beast of the field and every bird of the sky, and brought *them* to the man to see what he would call them; and whatever the man called a living creature, that was its name. [20] The man gave names to all the cattle, and to the birds of the sky, and to every beast of the field, but for Adam there was not found a helper suitable for him. [21] So the Lord God caused a deep sleep to fall upon the man, and he slept; then He took one of his ribs and closed up the flesh at that place. [22] The Lord God fashioned into a woman the rib which He had taken from the man, and brought her to the man. [23] The man said, "This is now bone of my bones, and flesh of my flesh; she shall be called Woman, because she was taken out of Man." [24] For this reason a man shall leave his father and his mother, and be joined to his wife; and they shall become one flesh. [25] And the man and his wife were both naked and were not ashamed.

The Fall of Man

In **Genesis 3:1-24** we can read: "Now the serpent was more crafty than any beast of the field which the Lord God had made. And he said to the woman, "Indeed, has God said, 'You shall not eat from any tree of the garden'?" ² The woman said to the serpent, "From the fruit of the trees of the garden we may eat; ³ but from the fruit of the tree which is in the middle of the garden, God has said, 'You shall not eat from it or touch it, or you will die.'" ⁴ The serpent said to the woman, "You surely will not die! ⁵ For God knows that in the day you eat from it your eyes will be opened, and you will be like God, knowing good and evil." ⁶ When the woman saw that the tree was good for food, and that it was a delight to the eyes, and that the tree was desirable to make *one* wise, she took from its fruit and ate; and she gave also to her husband with her, and he ate. ⁷ Then the eyes of both of them were opened, and they knew that they were naked; and they sewed fig leaves together and made themselves loin coverings. ⁸ They heard the sound of the Lord God walking in the garden in the cool of the day, and the man and his wife hid themselves from the presence of the Lord God among the trees of the garden. ⁹ Then the Lord God called to the man, and said to him, "Where are you?" ¹⁰ He said, "I heard the sound of You in the garden, and I was afraid because I was naked; so I hid myself." ¹¹ And He said, "Who told you that you were naked? Have you eaten from the tree of which I commanded you not to eat?" ¹² The man said, "The woman whom You gave *to be* with me, she gave me from the tree, and I ate." ¹³ Then the Lord God said to the woman, "What is this you have done?" And the woman said, "The serpent deceived me, and I ate." ¹⁴ The Lord God said to the serpent, "Because you have done this, Cursed are you more than all cattle, and more than every beast of the field; on your belly you will go, and dust you will eat all the days of your life; ¹⁵ and I will put enmity between you and the woman, and between your seed and her seed; He shall bruise you on the head, and you shall bruise him on the heel." ¹⁶ To the woman He said, "I will greatly multiply your labor in childbirth, in labor you will bring forth children; yet your desire will be for your husband, and he will rule over you." ¹⁷ Then to Adam He said, "Because you have listened to the voice of your wife, and have eaten from the tree about which I commanded you, saying, 'You shall not eat from it'; cursed is the ground because of you; in labor you will eat of it all the days of your life. ¹⁸ "Both thorns and thistles it shall grow for you; and you will eat the plants of the field;

¹⁹ By the sweat of your face You will eat bread, till you return to the ground, because from it you were taken; for you are dust, and to dust you shall return." ²⁰ Now the man called his wife's name Eve, because she was the mother of all *the* living. ²¹ The Lord God made garments of skin for Adam and his wife, and clothed them. ²² Then the Lord God said, "Behold, the man has become like one of Us, knowing good and evil; and now, he might stretch out his hand, and take also from the tree of life, and eat, and live forever"— ²³ therefore the Lord God sent him out from the garden of Eden, to cultivate the ground from which he was taken. ²⁴ So He drove the man out; and at the east of the garden of Eden He stationed the cherubim and the flaming sword which turned every direction to guard the way to the tree of life.

I was sharing that because man was disobedient to God he would not be content with all of his work—because his heart should belong to the Lord. So he prayed with me and gave his heart to the Lord and Savior. A week later his wife invited Christ into her heart, and later on her sister-in-law accepted Christ. After that he invited his friend to his home to eat together and many people heard the Gospel through this man, and now he has two children. All the glory and honor be to Him who saved the people.

Ibrahim's Testimony

While we were attending a prayer meeting at our friend's house the phone rang, and my friend's wife picked up the phone. It was the nurse from Stevens Hospital who asked her if she knew a man named Ibrahim, whose family name matched that of my friend and his wife. She responded that she did not know him.

When she told us the story, we called the hospital and asked what the situation was with him, and the nurse told us that Ibrahim had tried to commit suicide. The police found him on the street and brought him to the hospital, and he did not feel good and was nearly unconscious. They had to wait until the next morning to see if his condition would improve.

The next day a friend of mine and I went to the hospital and saw him lying on a bed in the CCU, unconscious. We stayed there and started to pray for him. Later on that same night, he started to move and there was hope for him to recover. So we went to see him and stood by his bed and he was grasping for us and asked who we were. I told him that we had been praying for him from the night before that the Lord would keep him alive. We assured him that we were there with him because we knew that the Lord loves him so much and was keeping him alive so that he could hear the gospel.

He asked me how I knew that the Lord loves him, I said to him that Jesus died for him on the cross and rose again on the third day. I told him that we have all sinned and fallen short of the glory of the Lord. I told him that Jesus is the light of the world. He then replied that he wanted us to hear his story.

He told us that he was highly educated in France, with a PHD in Mathematics. During the course of his studies, he met an exchange student from the United States, and he fell in love with his daughter, and they married. Afterward, he decided to move his new family to the States and settled in Colorado. He tried to find a job at the university but was not successful as he could not hold a normal conversation in English. So he started to work with three other Iranians who had received a permit to open a carpet cleaning business. Because he did not have a work permit, he paid them in cash. After three months the income in their carpet cleaning company was steadily increasing. His business companions told him to leave the shop, or they would call the immigration office and let them know he was working illegally.

Ibrahim went home and told his family that he had lost his money and that there were no other jobs available for him. His family blamed Ibrahim and told him that because he did not have a work permit in the States, there was nothing that they could do for him. Ibrahim was so depressed and didn't know what to do.

A few months later, another friend of Ibrahim encouraged him go to Seattle where there is a lot of rain. He could open another carpet cleaning business and be successful there. Ibrahim then decided to go to Seattle and found three other Iranians who agreed to start a shop with him. After three months they treated him the same way his previous friends did. So he felt helpless and did not know what to do.

These friends in Seattle had rented a small studio for Ibrahim where he could live. He left the shop, went to his studio and was feeling totally hopeless. He was still clueless as to what he should be doing. He decided to write a note in which he expressed that he felt unworthy to be a father or a husband. Consequently, he decided to take an overdose of sleeping pills and was in bed waiting to die. A few minutes later, he was so thirsty that he went toward the refrigerator to drink some water. The moment he opened the door of the refrigerator a light shone on his face, and he fell down.

His studio was next to the apartment manager's office, so she heard the loud noise when Ibrahim fell down. She opened the door to his studio and saw that he was lying on the floor. She became afraid and called Ibrahim's friend that had rented out his studio to Ibrahim. The friend came and when he and the woman saw that Ibrahim had tried to commit suicide, they dragged his body outside on the ground and left him at the side of the street so that the Police later could find him and bring him to the hospital.

Ibrahim asked me how I could say that the Lord loves him. I said to him: "Jesus loves you so much that he did not let you die before you could hear the good news that Jesus died on the cross for you and rose again on the third day, and by believing in him you will receive the forgiveness of your sins and you will have eternal life and will be with him forever." Ibrahim made it clear that as I said that Jesus is the light of the world, he would like to give his life to the Lord Jesus Christ and accept Him as his Lord and Savior.

I prayed with him and a few hours later his doctor showed up and said to him: "Ibrahim, are you ready to attempt suicide again?" He responded with a no. The doctor asked why he had attempted it before. Ibrahim then said: "My body is the temple of the Lord." It is amazing that Ibrahim had never read the Bible, and now he tells his doctor that his body is the temple of God. That could only have been revealed to Ibrahim by The Holy Spirit. Then the doctor asked him how much 2+2 is? He said "4." Then the doctor asked him how much 3+4 is. Ibrahim said "7." I started to laugh because the doctor did not know that he was educated and had a degree in mathematics.

The next day Ibrahim was discharged from the hospital, and I took him to our apartment to stay with us. I called his wife and shared the course of events with her, and Ibrahim's son-in-law came from Colorado and gave him a ride home. His wife started to thank me, and I told her that she should thank God who has saved her husband, and I told her that he is a believer in Jesus Christ and that Jesus not only saved his soul but also his body. Then I shared the gospel with her and she accepted Jesus Christ.

The next day her daughter called and started to thank me. Again, when I spoke with her, I shared the gospel of the Lord Jesus Christ and she accepted Jesus Christ into her heart too. When Ibrahim arrived at his home and knocked on the door, his wife and his daughter said to him that they also had become Christians and that they were excited. Later, they invited me and my friend to Colorado, and I attended his baptism. It was a unique day. He was crying and sharing his testimony, and all of the people in the church were blessed.

A few months later he and his wife called me. He had written a song to the Lord, and he and his wife were singing and praising the Lord together. He wrote many other beautiful songs to the Lord also. Pretty soon, he became continually active at the church over there. A few years later he passed away. I really miss him, but I know that one day, I will see him in heaven.

I would like to point out some important elements that led to Ibrahim getting help in the difficult situation he was in. First of all, God used that nurse to call us. Then we followed up by beginning to pray for him and, praise the Lord, we were persistent in prayer. There is power in prayer because Jesus said: "Truly, I say to you, if you ask the Father for anything in My name, He will give it to you." (John 16:23 NASB 1995)

There are many people that are ready to receive the Lord in their hearts. It is our responsibility to reach out to these people, to pray for them, and to share the good news so they may truly know that Jesus loves them and died for them. When they put their trust in the Lord Jesus and receive him, their sins will be forgiven.

Sometimes we do not know why we go through hard times in our life. We need to learn by experience that the Lord can turn around that situation for good, even as happened to Ibrahim. He was not unique to the Lord. God wants you also to experience his goodness. The Bible says that "the goodness of God leads you to repentance." **(Romans 2:4 NKJV)**. Just be open when you hear the good news of salvation. Do not say that you are OK and that the Gospel is not good for you, because it is written in the Bible: "for all have sinned and fall short of the glory of God." **(Romans 3:23 NKJV)**.

Also, I would like to encourage you not to miss the opportunities that the Lord brings into your life to share the Gospel with people. Use every moment that God gives you for His glory and do not say that someone else can do it. Yes, of course, if you are disobedient, the Lord will use someone else, but there is no benefit in missing out on golden opportunities to share the gospel.

Our God is not handicapped, so that he cannot reach out to people, but He wants to bless you and use you as a coworker with Him to advance his kingdom, so please do not miss the opportunities that he puts in your way. Use every second of your life wisely so that it may count for His glory. Also, remember that when Ibrahim got saved, his wife and daughter received the Lord, too.

Do not be afraid

One day I went to our Sunday morning church service. A lady inquired whether I could speak Arabic, and I wanted to l know why she asked. She responded that she met a young man from Iraq that was working at a gas station and she gave him a Bible and asked him to start reading from the Gospel of John. Two years later she went to the same gas station and saw that man again. She asked if he had read the Gospel of John and he responded affirmatively.

Now she wanted to know if I could speak Arabic, so that I would be able to share the Gospel in his native language. I asked her if I could have his phone number. She gave it to me and I called him. His name was Hussein, and I promised that I would be seeing him the following Wednesday. The night before I wanted to go and see Hussein, I received a phone message from his roommate that if I would go and share the Gospel with him, they would kill me.

My sons checked the phone message and pleaded with me not to go to Hussein's home. They reminded me that there was a death threat over me if I would share the gospel with him.

When Wednesday arrived, I decided to go anyway. On the way back from work I did not return home. Instead, I went directly to Hussein's house and knocked on the door. He came out to greet me. In his place I saw pictures of people like Ayatollah Khomeini, the leader of the Iranian revolution, Muammar Muhammad Abu Minyar al-Gaddafi, commonly known as Colonel Gaddafi, the president of Libya, and others like him. Hussein asked if I had heard the message from his roommate that his friends would kill me if I dared to come in. I asked him where they were and he said that they had left three minutes earlier and that they may come back soon. He suggested that we should go somewhere else, so at approximately 7 PM we went to Dairy Queen, and I was able to share the Gospel with Him.

I quoted **Romans 3:23** which states that we all have sinned and fallen short of the glory of God. I also read **Romans 6:23** which tells us that the wages of sin is death. I asked him if it made sense to him and he said yes. I also asked what he would say to God If he would die that night. He did not know. I told him that God loves the world so much that he gave His only begotten son for us to die on the cross to pay the penalty for our sins **(John3:16)**.

John 3:16:
[16] "For God so loved the world, that He gave His only begotten Son, that whoever believes in Him shall not perish, but have eternal life.

I told him what the Bible says that Jesus Christ is the gift of God to us: [9] that if you confess with your mouth Jesus *as* Lord, and believe in your heart that God raised Him from the dead, you will be saved; [10] for with the heart a person believes, resulting in righteousness, and with the mouth he confesses, resulting in salvation. [11] For the Scripture says that: "Whoever believes in Him will not be disappointed." **(Romans 10:9-11)**.

I shared John 14:6 with him.

John 14:6:
[6] Jesus said to him, "I am the way, and the truth, and the life; no one comes to the Father but through Me."

I asked him, "Would you like to invite Jesus as your Lord and savior and asked Him to forgive your sins?" He said yes, and He invited Jesus Christ as his only Lord and Savior into his heart. I was sharing the assurance of salvation to him as the Bible says:

1 John 5:3:
These things I have written to you who believe in the name of the Son of God, so that you may know that you have eternal life.

John 1:12:
But as many as received Him, to them He gave the right to become children of God, even to those who believe in His name.

Subsequently, I told him that following and obeying the Lord on a daily basis is a moment-by-moment decision.

The Bible says:

Matthew 28:19-20:
[9] Go therefore and make disciples of all the nations, baptizing them in the name of the Father and the Son and The Holy Spirit, [20] teaching them to observe all that I commanded you; and lo, I am with you always, even to the end of the age."

Hussein was so excited that he got saved and wanted to be obedient to the Lord, so he asked me to baptize him at 11 PM the same night that he got saved. I called my family and told them the story of Hussein and asked them to join me as I was going to baptize him, so my family came to the Church and around midnight, I baptized Hussein. All the glory and honor be to Jesus.

Two years later, I was downtown Seattle with an evangelistic outreach group in front of the Westgate Mall. I saw two men standing at the cross section to go into the mall, and The Holy Spirit guided me to go and share the Gospel with them. I asked them if they knew what we were doing there. One responded and asked me how I dared to worship God with music and instruments. I asked him if he was Muslim.

He confirmed that he was a Muslim and that he had never worshiped

Allah with Music. I wanted him to know that the Lord had changed my life and given me the privilege of calling the creator my Heavenly Father. I worship Him with many instruments and with joy.

Psalm 150 contains a short and comprehensive description on ways in which we may praise God:

Psalm 150:
1 Praise the LORD! Praise God in His sanctuary; Praise Him in His mighty expanse. 2 Praise Him for His mighty deeds; Praise Him according to His excellent greatness. 3 Praise Him with trumpet sound; Praise Him with harp and lyre. 4 Praise Him with tambourine and dancing; Praise Him with stringed instruments and flute. 5 Praise Him with loud cymbals; Praise Him with resounding cymbals. 6 Everything that has breath shall praise the LORD. Praise the LORD!

The Muslims in the Seattle mall tried to put me down because I had rejected Islam and become a Christian. I told them that the Lord had changed me and he could change them, too. I shared the Gospel with them, and both of them repented and gave their lives to the Lord Jesus Christ and invited Him into their hearts.

I gave them Bibles, and one of them asked me to write my name inside the Bible. I told them that they did not need my name but only the name of Jesus. Later, I disclosed to them that my name was Mark.

The moment I mentioned my name they started crying. I apologized and asked if I had said anything hurtful to them. In return, they asked if I knew any Muslims from Iraq named Hussein. I said yes, and they told me that they were the friends of Hussein who had left a death threat message on my home phone.

I was on my knees and I said: "Thank you, Lord, that you removed fear from me and that I was obedient to you and shared your Gospel with Hussein, and now those people who wanted to kill me are my brothers in Christ." All the glory and honor be unto you Lord.

In the word of God (The Bible) we are admonished not to be afraid 366 times.

Psalm 27:1 says
1 [A Psalm] of David. The LORD is my light and my salvation; Whom should I fear? The LORD is the defense of my life; Whom should I dread?

Psalm 23 says
1 A Psalm of David. The LORD is my shepherd, I will not be in need. 2 He lets me lie down in green pastures; He leads me beside quiet waters. 3 He restores my soul; He guides me in the paths of righteousness for the sake of His name. 4 Even though I walk through the valley of the shadow of death, I fear no evil, for You are with me; Your rod and Your staff, they comfort me. 5 You prepare a table before me in the presence of my enemies; You have anointed my head with oil; My cup overflows. 6 Certainly goodness and faithfulness will follow me all the days of my life, and my dwelling [will be] in the house of the LORD forever.

The Bible says that today is the day of salvation, so you can invite Jesus into your heart right now and become a child of God.

God Can Speak to You Through a Boy

Shortly after I got saved in 1993, the Lord anointed me to share the Gospel with the lost. Because I did a lot of street evangelism, my wife and I regularly went to Vancouver in British Columbia where we had an outreach ministry to the Iranian people. A pastor in a local church from Seattle was with me and a young boy by the name of Daniel, who was a relative of the pastor. The night before we went there, I asked Daniel what he was going to do the next day; he told me the pastor told him that he would go with Mark to Vancouver to share the Gospel with the Iranians.

Daniel asked him, "why not go to Gastown in Vancouver to share the Gospel over there?" The pastor suggested to me that we should first go to Gastown and later up to North Vancouver, as Daniel had said to him earlier. I agreed, and so we went to Gastown and I started to share the gospel with several people. They were not ready to receive Christ, however, so we decided to walk down the street.

We ended up at a Persian carpet store. The moment we arrived at the store, the salesman displayed an ignorant attitude and distanced himself from us. Finally, he came back and asked how he could help us. I told him that we were not there to buy anything, but that we wanted to let him know how much God loves him. I asked the pastor if he would go back to the car and bring a Bible. Then I told the salesman that God loves him so much that he gave His only begotten son to die on the cross for him. Suddenly, the salesman started to cry, and he said he had two sons and that they were twins. One of them whose name was Daniel was suffering from pneumonia and was lying in a coma in the hospital. I told the salesman that while we were in Seattle, my friend Daniel had suggested that we should go to Gastown. I was then reflecting over the fact that the salesman's son who was in the hospital had the same name as my friend.

I asked the salesman if he knew that Jesus could heal his son if he would believe in Him. I then offered to pray for his son's healing and he said, "Please do it." I cried out to the Lord and said: "Lord, you healed so many people and you even raised a man from the dead after 4 days. You are the same God yesterday, today, and forever, so would you please heal this sick boy, Daniel, for your glory." I was on my knees for about half an hour. Then the salesman told me that he was a Muslim and was wondering what he should say to his son if he got healed. I told him that he first needed to invite Jesus Christ as his Lord and Savior into his heart and believe that He is the only son of God. Consider the word of God according to the Gospel of John chapter 1:1-14:

The Deity of Christ:
In the beginning was the Word, and the Word was with God, and the Word was God. [2] He was in the beginning with God. [3] All things came into being through Him, and apart from Him nothing came into being that has come into being. [4] In Him was life, and the life was the Light of men. [5] The Light shines in the darkness, and the darkness did not comprehend it. **(John 1:1-5 NASB 1995).**

The Witness John:
[6] There came a man sent from God, whose name was John. [7] He came as a witness, to testify about the Light, so that all might believe through him. [8] He was not the Light, but *he came* to testify about the Light. [9] There was the true Light which, coming into the world,

enlightens every man. ¹⁰ He was in the world, and the world was made through Him, and the world did not know Him. ¹¹ He came to His own, and those who were His own did not receive Him. ¹² But as many as received Him, to them He gave the right to become children of God, *even* to those who believe in His name, ¹³ who were born, not of blood nor of the will of the flesh nor of the will of man, but of God. **(John 1:6-13 NASB 1995)**.

The Word Made Flesh:
"¹⁴ And the Word became flesh, and dwelt among us, and we saw His glory, glory as of the only begotten from the Father, full of grace and truth." **(John 1:14 NASB 1995)**.

John 14:1-6:
"Do not let your heart be troubled; believe in God, believe also in Me. ² In My Father's house are many dwelling places; if it were not so, I would have told you; for I go to prepare a place for you. ³ If I go and prepare a place for you, I will come again and receive you to Myself, that where I am, *there* you may be also. ⁴ And you know the way where I am going." ⁵ Thomas said to Him, "Lord, we do not know where You are going, how do we know the way?" ⁶ Jesus said to him, "I am the way, and the truth, and the life; no one comes to the Father but through Me.

Romans 10:9-11:
that if you confess with your mouth Jesus *as* Lord, and believe in your heart that God raised Him from the dead, you will be saved; ¹⁰ for with the heart a person believes, resulting in righteousness, and with the mouth he confesses, resulting in salvation. ¹¹ For the Scripture says "Whoever believes in Him will not be disappointed."

I told the salesman that he could invite Jesus into his heart as the word of God said. "You will be saved and then Jesus said that you may ask in his name and you shall receive it. After you get saved you can pray for you sons in Jesus' name and the Lord will hear your prayer." So the salesman prayed and received Christ.

As I was praying, I saw a vision of his son Daniel and he was wearing a white robe sitting on his bed and eating, I shared my vison with the salesman and I told him that his son had been healed. The salesman said that he hoped so, and I told him not to doubt it, and that God is able, and he did it.

I got the phone number for the shop as we left. The next day I called and someone else picked up the phone. I asked him where the other salesman was and he said that he was at the hospital. I inquired how the sick boy was doing and requested the phone number for Daniel's father. I then called him and he said: "Mark, when I went to the hospital last night, I saw my son wearing a white robe, sitting on the bed and eating. I asked my wife what had happened. She explained to me that the day before at 1 PM he was sitting on the bed after they changed his clothes. He said that he was hungry. The salesman asked me if I remembered that on the previous day, I had shared my vision with him. I responded to him by saying: "Praise the Lord. He is a Mighty God." A few weeks after my visit at their home Daniel was healthy and playing with his brother.

I give all the glory and honor to the Lord Jesus Christ, for what happened in the healing of Daniel, the salesman's son. I am also thankful to God that my friend Daniel from Seattle had suggested that we should go to Gastown and share the Gospel. God was using this course of events and guiding us to do works that he had prepared in advance for us. I therefore strongly encourage you to study the word of God and mentally prepare yourself so that you, too, may hear God's voice when he speaks to you, even through a young boy.

1 Samuel 3:1-21:
1 Now the boy Samuel was attending to the service of the LORD before Eli. And word from the LORD was rare in those days; visions were infrequent. 2 But it happened at that time as Eli was lying down in his place (now his eyesight had begun to be poor [and] he could not see [well],] 3 and the lamp of God had not yet gone out, and Samuel was lying down in the temple of the LORD where the ark of God [was,] 4 that the LORD called Samuel; and he said, "Here I am." 5 Then he ran to Eli and said, "Here I am, for you called me." But he said, "I did not call, go back [and] lie down." So he went and lay down. 6 And the LORD called yet again, "Samuel!" So Samuel got up and went to Eli and said, "Here I am, for you called me." But he said, "I did not call, my son, go back [and] lie down." 7 Now Samuel did not yet know the LORD, nor had the word of the LORD yet been revealed to him. 8 So

the LORD called Samuel again for the third time. And he got up and went to Eli and said, "Here I am, for you called me." Then Eli realized that the LORD was calling the boy. 9 And Eli said to Samuel, "Go lie down, and it shall be if He calls you, that you shall say, 'Speak, LORD, for Your servant is listening.'" So Samuel went and lay down in his place. 10 Then the LORD came and stood, and called as at [the] other times: "Samuel! Samuel!" And Samuel said, "Speak, for Your servant is listening." 11 Then the LORD said to Samuel, "Behold, I am going to do a thing in Israel, [and] both ears of everyone who hears [about] it will ring. 12 "On that day I will carry out against Eli everything that I have spoken in regard to his house, from beginning to end. 13 "For I have told him that I am going to judge his house forever for the wrongdoing that he knew, because his sons were bringing a curse on themselves and he did not rebuke them. 14 "Therefore I have sworn to the house of Eli that the wrongdoing of Eli's house shall never be atoned for by sacrifice or offering." 15 So Samuel lay down until morning. Then he opened the doors of the house of the LORD. But Samuel was afraid to tell the vision to Eli. 16 Then Eli called Samuel and said, "Samuel, my son." And he said, "Here I am." 17 He said, "What is the word that He spoke to you? Please do not hide it from me. May God do the same to you, and more so, if you hide a [single] word from me of all the words that He spoke to you!" 18 So Samuel told him everything and hid nothing from him. And he said, "He is the LORD; let Him do what seems good to Him." 19 Now Samuel grew, and the LORD was with him, and He let none of his words fail. 20 And all Israel from Dan even to Beersheba knew that Samuel was confirmed as a prophet of the LORD. 21 And the LORD appeared again at Shiloh, because the LORD revealed Himself to Samuel at Shiloh by the word of the LORD.

Power of Prayer

As I mentioned above, my wife and I used to go street evangelizing in Vancouver, BC. One day we were walking on Lions Dale Street in North Vancouver, distributing tracts. I saw a man sitting in a wheel chair in front of a shop and I handed him a tract called "Peace with God." It was written in the Farsi language. After a while, The Holy Spirit prompted me to go back and ask him if he had any questions about the tract. I was obedient to The Holy Spirit and asked the man if he had any questions about the tract that I had just given to him. He answered affirmatively and requested that I explain the content of the tract to him. I shared the scripture which states that we all have sinned and fall short of the glory of God. **Romans 3:23:** "For all have sinned and fall short of the glory of God." And **Romans 6:23:** "For the wages of sin is death, but the free gift of God is eternal life in Christ Jesus our Lord."

I asked him if it made sense and he said yes. Then I told him that Jesus had said about himself that he is the Truth, the Way and the Life and that no one comes to the father except through him.

John14:6: Jesus said to him, "I am the way, and the truth, and the life; no one comes to the Father but through Me."

In **Romans 10:9**, it is written: "if you confess with your mouth Jesus *as* Lord, and believe in your heart that God raised Him from the dead, you will be saved." I asked him if he would like to repent and invite Jesus Christ into his heart as his Lord and Savior and he said yes.

Glory be to God. I prayed with him, and he asked me what my name was, and I told him. At the very moment when I said Mark, he started to cry and picked up his phone book and showed me where he had written my name. He said that he was living in Toronto, Canada, and a pastor of an Iranian church over there was his friend. This pastor had invited him to join his church for the last several years. He had never asked Christ into his heart, and a few months earlier he had moved to Vancouver. The pastor from Toronto told him that he had heard about me and gave him my name. He let him know that I shared the gospel in North Vancouver, mostly during weekends, and that he was praying he could see me. So this man concluded that this meeting must be a blessing from God. I told him, "I praise the Lord for that pastor who was praying for you for years; please call him and tell him you are saved. Thank him for years of prayer."

John16:23 says: "In that day you will not question Me about anything. Truly, truly, I say to you, if you ask the Father for anything in My name, He will give it to you."

A few months later I was in Vancouver attending at Iranian gathering because of Sisdah Bedar—the thirteen days after the Iranian New Year on March 21. Thousands of Iranians were there, and I saw the man moving with the wheelchair and distributing a video about Jesus and the Bible in Iranian. This reminds me of the Great Commission in the book of Matthew: "Go therefore and make disciples of all the nations, baptizing them in the name of the Father and the Son and The Holy Spirit, [20] teaching them to observe all that I commanded you; and lo, I am with you always, even to the end of the age." **(Matthew 28:10-20)**

Please keep praying for those who have heard the Gospel that they may get saved.

Use Every Opportunity

One Saturday my wife and I were sharing the GOSPEL with Iranians in Vancouver, BC. As my wife was walking and distributing tracts on one side of Lions Dale Street and I was doing the same thing on the other side, I found that my wife was talking to three Iranian ladies, I heard her talking about Jesus Christ. One of them loudly said that she herself was God. At this time, I joined my wife and I told the Lady that I heard what she had said. At this moment I kneeled in front of her and I gave her a challenge. I asked her if she would please look at the sun and tell the earth to stop and not to turn around the sun. She said that she could not do it. I opened the Bible and told her that I believed that through God one can do it. I read the story about Joshua for her.

Joshua 10:12-14:
12 Then Joshua spoke to the LORD on the day when the LORD turned the Amorites over to the sons of Israel, and he said in the sight of Israel, "Sun, stand still at Gibeon, And moon, at the Valley of Aijalon!" 13 So the sun stood still, and the moon stopped, Until the nation avenged themselves of their enemies. Is it not written in the Book of Jashar? And the sun stopped in the middle of the sky and did not hurry to go [down] for about a whole day. 14 There was no day like that before it or after it, when the LORD listened to the voice of a man; for the LORD fought for Israel.

She was amazed. Then I asked her and her two daughters if they still thought that she was God. They said no, and then I shared the Gospel with them. I asked if they would like to receive the Lord Jesus Christ as their Lord and Savior. All of them said yes and they prayed with us and invited Jesus Christ into their hearts as their only Lord and Savior. All glory and honor be to Him that saves them.

Serving the Lord in Austria

I used to go to Austria to share the Gospel with Iranian and Afghan refugees, and every year many of them heard the Gospel. The Holy Spirit changed their hearts. and they got saved.

One night about fifty people came to center where we were, and I was sharing the message that we all have sinned and fall short of the glory of God. After the meeting I invited the people to reassemble on the second floor for a teaching session, so that they could bring up any relevant questions about the message I had given.

During the question-and-answer session, a young man by the name of Mostafa, seemed to display quite a bit of anger. He asked me if even Mohammad, the Muslim prophet, is a sinner. I shared Romans 3:23 with him, wherein it is clearly stated that all have sinned and fall short of the Glory of God. This also includes Mohammad and everyone needs a savior, Jesus Christ. Also, in John 14:6 we may read that no one comes to the Father except through Him. He got truly angry and left the class.

I was praying for him that night and asked the Lord to touch his heart. The next evening our teaching session was scheduled to start at 6 PM and I was walking inside of the classroom and praying that The Holy Spirit would bring more people to us who could hear about Jesus.

At 5 PM Mostafa was knocking on the door and I opened it and told him that class would start at 6. He let me know that he had a question and that he could not sleep during the night. He had discovered that what I was teaching was the truth and he wanted to give his life to Jesus. Consequently, he prayed with me and invited Jesus as Lord and Savior into his heart. Mostafa was one of hundreds of people who gave their lives to Jesus.

All glory and honor be to Jesus. They were without hope and now they have a living hope.

Mission Trip to Norway

I went to Norway by the invitation from a friend of mine. One day while doing street evangelism passing out tracts, a man with his bike came up to me. He was very angry; he slapped the tract on my face, and asked me where God was. I said, "Right here." He said that the wife of one of his friends had been killed by someone and that his friend was very depressed. The man encouraged his friend to go and kill his wife's murderer. I told him that this could make the widowed husband even sadder. He would be thinking about what had happened to his wife and possibly also suffer from inner pain for killing someone.

He asked me what he should do. I told him that it would be better for him to give his life to Jesus and then he could be filled with The Holy Spirit. This would enable him to have a personal relationship with the Lord in prayer and worship. Then he could go to his friend with the joy of the Lord and worship Him while they would be together. I told him, "He may ask you what has happened to you and you can tell him that only Jesus can give you peace."

He said that was a good idea. So I shared the Gospel with him, and he prayed with me and received Christ as his only Lord and Savior. He asked me for tracts so that he could share the message of salvation with his friend. All glory be to our Lord Jesus Christ. I encourage you to ask the Lord to give you wisdom so that you may know how you can share the Gospel with people.

Iranians were not Muslim

1400 years ago, Iranians were not Muslim and Islam was forcefully introduced as a religion. The perpetrators killed millions of people and forced many Iranians to become Muslim. The Quran is written in Arabic, but the Iranian language is Farsi. The Leaders of Islam believe that the Quran should only be read in Arabic. In some cases, they have been forcing Iranians to read the Quran, in Arabic, though they don't understand it.

Normally, Iranians will hear statements read from the Quran in Arabic three times in their lifetime. The first time is usually 6 to 8 days after their birth. The second time is when a couple is getting married—a religious man will read some verses from the Quran. Most likely, they will not understand those verses because they are written in Arabic. Also, most young couples want their wedding ceremony to go quickly. The third time when verses from the Quran are read to a Muslim is in the presence of someone who has just died, before the body is taken away for burial.

A common fact among Muslims is that very few of those who begin to read the Quran and memorize it actually understand the meaning of its content. Yet, when presented with the Gospel, many are fearful to accept Christ because Satan is using the doctrine of Muslim leaders to instigate fear in those who reject Islam. They are taught that Allah will send them to hell and their family will reject them, too. Also, in the Quran, there are many verses that may propagate fear to those who reject Islam. The most severe doctrine that Muslims have to live under is the threat that they will be killed if they become Christians.

John 10:9-10:
In this scripture verse Jesus says of himself: "⁹ I am the door; if anyone enters through Me, he will be saved, and will go in and out and find pasture. ¹⁰ The thief comes only to steal and kill and destroy; I came that they may have life, and have *it* abundantly."

The abundant life that we may have in knowing Jesus Christ is the reason why I plead with Muslims not to fear. I say to them, "If you believe in Christ, the Lord will use you to save your family." I encourage them to read the history of Persia and how the Lord blessed Iranians. Here is what the Bible declares about King Cyrus:

God Uses Cyrus

Isaiah 45:1-7:
1 "Thus says the LORD to His anointed, To Cyrus, whose right hand I have held--To subdue nations before him And loose the armor of kings, To open before him the double doors, So that the gates will not be shut: 2 'I will go before you And make the crooked places straight; I will break in pieces the gates of bronze And cut the bars of iron. 3 I will give you the treasures of darkness And hidden riches of secret places, That you may know that I, the LORD, Who call [you] by your name, [Am] the God of Israel. 4 For Jacob My servant's sake, And

Israel My elect, I have even called you by your name; I have named you, though you have not known Me. 5 I [am] the LORD, and [there is] no other; [There is] no God besides Me. I will gird you, though you have not known Me, 6 That they may know from the rising of the sun to its setting That [there is] none besides Me. I [am] the LORD, and [there is] no other; 7 I form the light and create darkness, I make peace and create calamity; I, the LORD, do all these [things].'

Throughout the Bible, we find servants of God who are anointed. As this Bible text indicates, King Cyrus is one such servant. If anyone would pose the question of whether Mohammad is called an anointed one, the answer would be quite obvious: of course not. You would not find any literary source that could validate such a claim.

Cyrus's Proclamation

Ezra 1:1-4:
Now in the first year of Cyrus king of Persia, in order to fulfill the word of the LORD by the mouth of Jeremiah, the LORD stirred up the spirit of Cyrus king of Persia, so that he sent a proclamation throughout his kingdom, and also put it in writing, saying: 2 "This is what Cyrus king of Persia says: 'The LORD, the God of heaven, has given me all the kingdoms of the earth, and He has appointed me to rebuild for Him a house in Jerusalem, which is in Judah. 3 'Whoever there is among you of all His people, may his God be with him! Go up to Jerusalem which is in Judah and rebuild the house of the LORD, the God of Israel; He is the God who is in Jerusalem. 4 'And every survivor, at whatever place he may live, the people of that place are to support him with silver and gold, with equipment and cattle, together with a voluntary offering for the house of God which is in Jerusalem.'"

A Great Harvest

Robert Bruce, a Scottish missionary to Iranian Muslims in the late 1800s, wrote home to his supporters, 'I am not reaping the harvest; I scarcely claim to be sowing the seed; I am hardly ploughing the soil, but I am gathering out the stones. That, too, is missionary work; let it be supported by loving sympathy and fervent prayer.' [1]

If only Bruce could see Iran now. By God's grace, we find ourselves in

a season of harvest:
- Hundreds of thousands of Iranians are turning to faith in Christ.
- Operation World continues to name Iran as having the fastest growing evangelical church in the world. [2]
- Despite continued intense pressure from the Islamic regime, more Iranians have become Christians in the last 20 years than in the previous 1,300 years since Islam came to Iran.

Revolution in Iran

What if I told you that the greatest Christian missionary in the history of Iran was a devout Muslim? You'd think I was crazy, or at the very least, a liar. But I've heard from more than one Iranian Christian over the past 20 years that the greatest missionary in the history of Iran — a history that predates Daniel in the Lion's Den — is the Grand Ayatollah Ruhollah Khomeini, the leader of the 1979 Islamic Revolution that ended 2,500 years of Persian monarchy in Iran. How is it, you may ask, that a radical Shiite Muslim would be Iran's greatest missionary for Christ?

Khomeini forced Iran's last Shah from power and ushered in Islamic rule. He was an expert in Sharia, or Islamic law. He put Islamic leaders, the mullahs, in charge of the whole country. He promised to replace corruption of the West-loving Shah with a government that would run the country according to true Islamic principles. It would be a paradise on Earth, he said, as if Muhammed himself were running things.

Forty years later, Iranians will tell you that the promised paradise hasn't materialized. Rampant corruption continues under the Revolutionary Guard Corps, the foot soldiers of the Islamic regime. The rate of drug addiction in Iran is one of the highest in the world. Iran's economy is in shambles, and in recent weeks Iranians across the country have taken to the streets in protest after the government raised gas prices and enacted strict rations. At least 200 Iranians have paid for the protests with their lives — and that number could be more than 1,000.

Remember: the Islamic government promised, and still claims, to run the country according to Islamic principles. The Supreme Leader says he gets instructions directly from Allah. But after 40 years, Iranians can see very clearly that the government Khomeini established doesn't work. So it's no great leap for Iranians to move from "Islamic government doesn't work" to a correlated truth: Islam doesn't work.

By some estimates, 70 percent of Iran's people have rejected Islam. If following the rules laid out by Muhammad doesn't work for a country, why would it work for an individual? Why should anyone continue to follow his teachings? Many Iranians have become atheists, rejecting the idea of any god. And thousands have tried to fill the void with drugs, illicit sex or money. But hundreds of thousands of Iranians — some estimate that even more than a million people—have found the True God, the One who sent His Son to pay the price for sin. He does not ask them to earn his favor by following a set of rules, but instead, he paid the price himself for their sins and failures.

Iranians are watching Christian TV shows via illegal but widely available satellite dishes. They are circumventing national firewalls to search the internet for online Bibles and other Christian content in Farsi. They are chatting online and even by phone with Farsi-speaking Christians in other nations, asking heart-questions and choosing, boldly, to leave behind the failed religion of their national leaders and instead embrace Jesus Christ, the Son of God.

In many Islamic countries, the cost for leaving Islam to follow Christ usually begins within the family. Parents might punish or even disown a child, or a sibling might threaten or pressure a brother or sister to return to Islam and stop bringing shame on the family. But in Iran that's not usually the case; if the parents don't think Islam works, they aren't likely to be angry when their child chooses a different path. Following Christ in Iran is not without cost, however. While parents might accept a child's decision to follow Christ, the heirs of Ayatollah Khomeini, the mullahs who currently run the Islamic Republic, certainly will not. All of the above-ground, public, "building" churches in Iran have been forced to close. The only Christian meetings still occurring are private, underground services. Every one of them is illegal, and Christians who meet together face arrest, torture and long prison sentences — especially the group leaders.

Christian women face sexual assault while in custody, and imprisoned

Christians are sometimes forced to sign over the deeds to their homes as bail, with the threat that if they continue Christian activities they will be re-arrested and their homes confiscated. The spiritual hunger in Iran has not been satisfied by 40 years of following Khomeini's path. And yet Khomeini prepared the way for the current revival. The Lord's promise in Jeremiah 49, that He would "set my throne in Elam," is coming true in our day. Our Persian Christian brothers and sisters have found a Bread of Life that truly satisfies, and they are determined to share Him with their countrymen. The cost of their work is high, but the need is great. So they continue to reach out, to share their faith, to pray for healing in Jesus' name or offer a Bible to a curious coworker.

Of course, they credit God for the fruitfulness and success of their Gospel work, pointing out that He is keeping His promise to establish His throne in their nation. But for preparing the soil, they also credit the founder of the Islamic Republic of Iran, the man who displayed the true face of Islam for every Iranian to see. Grand Ayatollah Ruhollah Khomeini: the greatest Christian missionary in the history of Iran.

"If we remain faithful to our calling, our conviction is that it is possible to see the nation transformed within our lifetime," one house church leader shared. "Because Iran is a strategic gateway nation, the growing church in Iran will impact Muslim nations across the Islamic world." And like the church of Acts shows us, the persecution that believers suffered as a group of committed disciples—inspired and ignited by The Holy Spirit—became a catalyst for the multiplication of believers and churches. When persecution came, the apostles didn't scatter but remained in the city where it was most strategic and most dangerous. They were arrested, shamed and beaten for their message. Still, they stayed to lay the foundations for an earth-shaking movement.

So it is in Iran. When the Iranian revolution of 1979 established a hardline Islamic regime, the next two decades ushered in a wave of persecution that continues today. All missionaries were kicked out, evangelism was outlawed, Bibles in the Persian or Farsi language were banned, and several pastors were killed. Many feared the small, fledgling Iranian church wouldn't survive.

Instead, the church, fueled by the devotion and passion of disciples, has multiplied exponentially. Iran has become the Muslim nation that is most open to the gospel. As the church in Iran multiplies, persecution follows. Over the last few months, Open Doors has learned about arrests of numerous Christians in Iran. The crackdown on house churches continues, as officials search for and arrest people involved in these typically, tiny fellowships. Iran's "no house church" law threatens prison sentences of varying lengths. Open Doors has reported numerous atrocities against Christians in Iranian prisons, infamous for their treatment of political prisoners. In 2019, at least 37 Christians were arrested: eight in Bushehr, nine in Rasht, 12 in Amol, two in Ahvaz, and one each in Hamedan, Shiraz and Isfahan.

On July 1, in the southwestern city of Bushehr, eight Christian converts, mostly in their 30s, were arrested, including five members of one family. Seven are still in prison, most likely in solitary confinement. Their homes were raided and Bibles confiscated, as well as Christian literature, wooden crosses and pictures with Christian symbols. Authorities also took laptops, phones, identity cards and bank cards. The officers are reported to have treated the Christians harshly, even though small children were present during the arrests. Also on April 16th, other converts from Bushehr reportedly lost their appeals against prison sentences for "propaganda activities against the regime through the formation of house churches."

In July 2019 another five converts were admitted to the central detention center in Karaj to begin their jail sentences, accused of "propaganda against the state." Manoto News broadcasted footage of these Christians, four of whom have young children. They were seen waving goodbye to their loved ones, suffering for the sake of the gospel in the Middle East.

After their arrests, the five were released in early 2018 after each posted a bail of 30 million tomans (around $7,000). In March 2019, Milad, Yaghoob, Shahebedin and Alireza were sentenced to four months in prison. Amin, who has already spent a year in prison for his religious activities, was given 14 months. Their appeals were rejected last month. Pray with us by name for all of these believers, recognizing that they represent only a handful of thousands of our brothers and sisters in Iran who have been threatened, arrested or imprisoned for turning to Jesus and following Him.

How to share the Gospel with Muslims

- Share the good news of Jesus Christ with the world (including Muslims)
- Look for Muslims whose hearts are open to receiving the good news
- Offer a Bible to those who are open
- Pray with a Muslim in the name of Jesus
- Love Muslims as God loves them in thoughts, words, and actions

Matthew 22:36-39:
"Teacher, which is the great commandment in the Law?" 37 And He said to him, "'You shall love the Lord your God with all your heart, and with all your soul, and with all your mind.' 38 This is the great and foremost commandment. 39 The second is like it, 'You shall love your neighbor as yourself.'

Psalm 96:2-3:
Sing to the Lord, bless His name; proclaim good tidings of His salvation from day to day. 3 Tell of His glory among the nations, His wonderful deeds among all the peoples.

- Pray for an open heart toward your Muslim neighbors, for God's wisdom and instruction, and that God would lead you to a Muslim He is drawing to Jesus
- Look for opportunities to engage with Muslims around you

Read Luke 10:5-7, John 6:44 and 1 Corinthians 12:3 (below). What insights do you find for sharing the Good News with Muslims around you?

Luke 10:5-7:
Whatever house you enter, first say, 'Peace be to this house.' 6 If a man of peace is there, your peace will rest on him; but if not, it will return to you. 7 Stay in that house, eating and drinking what they give you; for the laborer is worthy of his wages. Do not keep moving from house to house.

John 6:44:
"No one can come to me unless the Father who sent me draws him; and I will raise him up on the last day."

1 Corinthians 12:3:
"Therefore I make known to you that no one speaking by the Spirit of God says, "Jesus is accursed"; and no one can say, "Jesus is Lord," except by The Holy Spirit."

- Prepare and memorize your own, two-sentence, Gospel presentation based on Romans 10:9. Look for opportunities to share this with Muslims around you

Romans 10:9:
that if you confess with your mouth Jesus as Lord, and believe in your heart that God raised Him from the dead, you will be saved;

- Memorize Mark 13:31, and practice out-loud. This is a good way to respond to the common hesitation that the Bible has been corrupted

Mark 13:31:
"Heaven and earth will pass away, but My words will not pass away."

Pray With People in the Name of Jesus

We covered:
1. Sharing the Gospel,
2. Finding a Person of Peace, and
3. Offering a Bible

Read Acts 3:1-10, and Mark 9:28-29. Consider the insights within these verses and how they might empower you to share Jesus with Muslims.

Acts 3:1-10 (KJV):
Now Peter and John were going up to the temple at the ninth hour, the hour of prayer. 2 And a man who had been lame from his mother's womb was being carried along, whom they used to set down every day at the gate of the temple which is called Beautiful, in order to beg alms

of those who were entering the temple. 3 When he saw Peter and John about to go into the temple, he began asking to receive alms. 4 But Peter, along with John, fixed his gaze on him and said, "Look at us!" 5 And he began to give them his attention, expecting to receive something from them. 6 But Peter said, "I do not possess silver and gold, but what I do have I give to you: In the name of Jesus Christ the Nazarene—walk!" 7 And seizing him by the right hand, he raised him up; and immediately his feet and his ankles were strengthened. 8 With a leap he stood upright and began to walk; and he entered the temple with them, walking and leaping and praising God. 9 And all the people saw him walking and praising God; 10 and they were taking note of him as being the one who used to sit at the Beautiful Gate of the temple to beg alms, and they were filled with wonder and amazement at what had happened to him.

Mark 9:28-29:
When He came into the house, His disciples began questioning Him privately, "Why could we not drive it out?" 29 And He said to them, "This kind cannot come out by anything but prayer."

- Prayerfully seek opportunities to engage with Muslims around you
- Pray with a Muslim (or any unbelieving friend) in Jesus' name

LOVE IN WORDS & ACTIONS

Read 1 John 4:7-5:5. Consider how the insights within these verses may be applicable in sharing the Good News with Muslims around you.

1 John 4:7-21:
Beloved, let us love one another, for love is from God; and everyone who loves is born of God and knows God. [8] The one who does not love does not know God, for God is love. [9] By this the love of God was manifested in us, that God has sent His only begotten Son into the world so that we might live through Him. 10 In this is love, not that we loved God, but that He loved us and sent His Son to be the propitiation for our sins. 11 Beloved, if God so loved us, we also ought to love one another. 12 No one has seen God at any time; if we love one another, God abides in us, and His love is perfected in us. 13 By

this we know that we abide in Him and He in us, because He has given us of His Spirit. 14 We have seen and testify that the Father has sent the Son to be the Savior of the world.

15 Whoever confesses that Jesus is the Son of God, God abides in him, and he in God. 16 We have come to know and have believed the love which God has for us. God is love, and the one who abides in love abides in God, and God abides in him. 17 By this, love is perfected with us, so that we may have confidence in the day of judgment; because as He is, so also are we in this world. 18 There is no fear in love; but perfect love casts out fear, because fear involves punishment, and the one who fears is not perfected in love. 19 We love, because He first loved us. 20 If someone says, "I love God," and hates his brother, he is a liar; for the one who does not love his brother whom he has seen, cannot love God whom he has not seen. 21 And this commandment we have from Him, that the one who loves God should love his brother also.

1 John 5:1-5:
Whoever believes that Jesus is the Christ is born of God, and whoever loves the Father loves the child born of Him. 2 By this we know that we love the children of God, when we love God and observe His commandments. 3 For this is the love of God, that we keep His commandments; and His commandments are not burdensome. 4 For whatever is born of God overcomes the world; and this is the victory that has overcome the world—our faith. 5 Who is the one who overcomes the world, but he who believes that Jesus is the Son of God?

More on Sharing the Gospel with Muslims

The testimony of the Gospels provides the most reliable witness to Christ. Preach the Gospel as it is! Do not soft-pedal around biblical terminology to please Muslim hearers. Be clear about what you believe and why you believe it. Know the Scriptures well, and know exactly what you believe. The more you know about your faith, the easier it is to talk with Muslims.

There is no gospel in Islam. The Qur'an clearly contradicts the essence of biblical Christianity and rejects the triune nature of God, disfigures the biblical doctrines of the person of Christ, and denies justification through faith on account of the work of Christ on the cross. While claiming to be the perpetual religion of nature and history, following in the footsteps of Christianity, it attempts to justify its claims by asserting that the Word of God, revealed in the New and Old Testament, is corrupted. Our apologetic discussion with Muslims should be to defend the Scriptures and prove that the Scriptures aren't corrupt as Muslims claim. Our goal is to open up their minds a bit so that they can start reading the Gospels for an eyewitness or a companion of an eyewitness to the real Jesus.

Always ask them the classic evangelistic questions. 'What about your salvation?' 'Can you be certain of this?' 'If you were to die, can you be certain you'd enter heaven at some point?' Their response is always, "No, I couldn't be certain, nor do I care."

Most western missionaries are results-oriented; instead, you should be concerned about preaching the Gospel correctly (as it is). The essence of Muslim evangelism is accurate communication about sin and grace: simply and clearly. Talk about the law and the gospel, not about infralapsarianism and divine simplicity! Don't compare the Bible with the Quran. That comes later!

Always remember that you are talking to Muslims. Avoid the use of Christian jargon. Speak about real sin, real guilt, and the reality of the power of the shed blood of Jesus! Do not be ashamed to use Jesus' direct and indirect titles clearly such as 'Son of God' 'Lamb of God' 'New Adam' 'I AM - YAHWEH' 'Savior' 'Almighty God.'

Use tact; be loving! Don't talk about reprobation with a Muslim or a new convert who just lost an unbelieving family member. Be kind and courteous! Many Muslims act and speak out of ignorance, not malice.

Be sensitive to their past - if they've had a bad experience with Christians, missionaries or churches, struggled with a particular sin etc., be understanding and compassionate! Muslims hate self-righteousness, and rightly so! Do not soft-pedal the law and the guilt of sin, but make sure they understand that you are a justified sinner, not a self-righteous "know it all" who is here to correct them!

Muslims will ask you many questions about your faith. Don't feel like you have to answer all of their questions in one day. However, make sure they hear your answers to one or two questions clearly. Stick with the subject - don't get sidetracked. When the conversation wanders, pull it back to center stage - the law and the gospel.

Muslims will ask you to comment on their faith. Don't go there; they will not benefit from your criticism (or feigned approval) of other religions. Your job isn't to debunk Islam but to give a clear witness to the truth of the Gospel. Instead of letting them drag you into the topic, turn the tables and ask them questions. Let them articulate their own understandings of the religious themes you are discussing; let what you communicate be the plain truth of Christian doctrines without enumerating how Islam is wrong.

The message of the Gospel offends Muslims. It is okay! Don't worry! God will take care of the hearer. It is His message. Muslims will not convert to Christ if they are not offended by the message of the Gospel. Offend them by being very clear about the teachings of Christ! Do not use any "Muslim friendly" Bible translations. "Muslim friendly" Bible translations are very deceptive! They are not true to the original Scriptures. Muslims see it as a form of deception by missionaries!

Muslim evangelism is not about winning an argument, but leading Muslims to Christ with the Gospel. Discussions may get heated and intense at times - that's okay. But the purpose of Muslim evangelism is not to show why you are right and Islam is wrong. It is to communicate the truth of the gospel! The message is to be the offence! Not you!

When Muslims are apathetic about sin - use the law. When Muslims have doubts or are skeptical - use basic apologetic arguments. When Muslims express guilt for sin - present the Gospel.

Evangelism is about leading Muslims to Christ. Convincing non-Christians or Evangelicals that Reformed theology is true, falls under the heading of *polemics*. Don't confuse the two.

When talking to Muslims stick with what all Christians hold in common wherever possible. Leave the internecine fighting among

Christians aside when talking to Muslims. A Muslim will not care so much about differences between the Catholics and the Protestants or Lutherans and Baptists. Issues such as the exact meaning of the Lord's Supper or methods of baptism should be addressed later, during discipleship!

Wherever possible, when talking to Muslims speak about Christianity as factually true - "Jesus did this," "Jesus said this," "people heard and saw him," etc. Keep away from the subjective line of approach-- "it works for me," "this is how I feel about it," "this is my testimony" Before meeting with your Muslim friends pray for wisdom.

Muslims will respect the text you quote, but not your personal opinion. Trust in the power of God. The Holy Spirit working through the word! Cite texts directly from the Scriptures with attribution. Jesus says, Paul says.... It will not help Muslims to hear your personal opinion on biblical issues. So, don't say "I think," or "it seems to me" or "I feel like…" Muslims interpret your thoughts, your take on things or your feelings as part of the corruption of the Bible.

Don't rush things with Muslims. Just because a Muslim is not ready to trust in Christ after one encounter does not mean that effective evangelism has not taken place. Pre-evangelism is equally vital. You may plant, but someone else may have to water! Always remember that it is not us who convert the Muslims to Christ but God Himself (in His time)!

Remember that evangelism isn't complete after you first present the Gospel message to a Muslim. Evangelism has to continue even after they repent and give their lives to Christ. They have to sit under the ministry of the Word. Evangelism of a Muslim is complete only after they are baptized, brought to the Lord's Supper and sat under the preaching of the Word at church. In other words, evangelism never ends.

Treat Muslims as objects of concern, not notches in your belt! Establish relationships and friendships with Muslims whenever and wherever possible.

Don't forget that a prophet is without honor in his own home. The chances of Muslim converts leading their own unbelieving family members (or someone close to them) to Christ by themselves are remote. Encourage them as they give witness to what they have learned, but also pray for God to bring other people into the picture to help evangelize their families.

Don't force things. If your Muslim friends balk, ridicule and otherwise are not interested, back off. Find another time and place. If after repeated attempts to communicate the gospel, someone still shows an unwillingness to hear what you have to say, "shake the dust off your feet and move on to a new town!"

Be willing to get your Muslim friends the resources they need: be willing to provide them with a Bible (not just a New Testament), the right book to read, and certainly an invitation to your home, and later an invitation to attend your church or to a Bible study, etc. Never ever use a Muslim friendly Bible translation. These translations are a product of some western mission agencies without any support from the national churches who know their context best.

Pray for opportunities to evangelize Muslims. Make sure to let your Muslim friends know that you regularly attend a church. Do not disconnect your evangelism effort from the church. Pray for your church - that God would bless the preaching of his word, that he would bring Muslims into our midst, and that he would bless the church with growth.

You don't have to become a practical Arminian to be a faithful evangelist! A Christian approach to Muslim evangelism simply means telling Muslims the truth in love without changing it. Trust that God The Holy Spirit will penetrate hearts and minds of Muslims with "the Gospel."

Muslims love to sing Islamic hymns that tell the stories of the Quran. Islamic hymn singing is singing the words of the Quran. Show your Muslim friends some samples of Christian biblical songs with verses directly taken from Scriptures. In other words, sing the Bible to them! The role of music in human culture is to join people together. Biblically we are commanded to sing the praises of Christ. There are 694 references to singing or music making in Holy Scriptures. Participatory singing is a very significant matter biblically. There will be no singing in Hell, but the saints in Heaven will sing everlastingly. That is really amazing and remarkable! Let us show Muslims what we will be doing in Heaven. "Fear God and give Him Glory, because the hour of His judgment has come, and Worship Him who made heaven and earth, the sea and the springs of water." **(Rev. 14:7)**

Enlightening the Misinformed

While it may have been the Apostle Paul who first preached the unadulterated gospel in Arabia and Damascus **(Gal. 1:15–17)**, the following centuries witnessed the introduction of various brands of Christianity ranging from orthodoxy to a number of heretical sects. Indeed, Eastern Christianity prior to the arrival of Muhammad—the prophet of Islam—was afflicted by internal divisions, theological disputes, and worship of saints and relics. Muhammad was exposed to unorthodox Jewish and Christian beliefs and practices in Arabia and later through his trading activities with Christians in the north. Consequently, he drew his conclusions about Christianity from distorted sources: Jewish heterodoxy and a mixture of Christian materials from biographies of saints and martyrs as well as the Apocrypha.

What is more significant is the fact that Muhammad and many generations of his followers have not had the Bible in their own language, and so they have not fully understood the message of the gospel. Instead, his colossal misunderstanding of true Christianity has been detrimental to the relationship between Islam and Christianity and has continued regrettably to our day.

In addition to these unfortunate factors, millions of Muslims are exposed to some ailing theological and spiritual teachings and practices of certain brands of churches in our day. So, it's no wonder that Muslims look upon the Christian faith and the Word of God with suspicion. It is the task of Christians to remain true to the gospel as the Apostle Paul was, so that by God's grace they might come to know Jesus Christ as Lord and Savior.

In other words, it is incumbent upon us to communicate to our Muslim friends the "true Truth" of God's glorious, self-revelation in

Christ, "in whom are hidden all the treasures of wisdom and knowledge" **(Col. 2:3)**. History and allegiance to the Word of God demand that the Church in our generation be committed to evangelize Muslims and to make such evangelism a priority if we are to see Muslims come to faith in Christ.

When Muhammad rejected Christ as communicated to him by early Christian heresies, he replaced Him and His gospel with an intensely legalistic system that will never transform the heart and satisfy the demands of the conscience (see **Heb. 9:9–10**). We can say of Muslims what Paul said of the Jews: "They have a zeal for God, but it is not according to knowledge" **(Rom. 10:2)**. Faithful missionaries to Muslims know for sure that only the power of the gospel can change the hearts of men and women. We need to be confident as we proclaim God's Word. We must spread His gospel in all its power across the world and make its proclamation a priority in our evangelism to Muslims **(Rom. 1:16–17)**.

More Helpful Suggestions

Remember that bearing witness to Christ is not an option for the Christian and must be verbal by its very nature. The communication of the gospel to an unbeliever is the joyful participation by the Christian in what God is doing in the world. Remember these encouraging words from Jesus: "By this my Father is gloried, that you bear much fruit" **(John 15:8)**. "Follow me, and I will make you become fishers of men" **(Mark 1: 17)**. "I am the way, and the truth, and the life. No one comes to the Father except through me" **(John 14:6)**. "But you will receive power when The Holy Spirit has come upon you, and you will be my witnesses in Jerusalem and in all Judea and Samaria, and to the ends of the earth" **(Acts 1:8)**. Toward this end, here are ten suggestions for sharing the gospel with your Muslim friend:

(1) Regard your Muslim friend as an individual who is in as much need of salvation as any other human being, including you. Every nonbeliever must be seen as a divine appointment sent to us by God. While some will not respond, others will come to faith in Christ. The Word of God says, "We are ambassadors for Christ, God making his appeal through us" **(2 Cor. 5:20)**.

(2) Make an effort to cultivate a genuine friendship with your Muslim neighbor and learn about his or her background.

(3) Show genuine Christian love in word and deed. One of my favorite missionaries to Muslims, who was martyred for his faith, is Raymond Lull. He traveled to North Africa during the bitter days of the Crusades and understood that the only way to overcome hostile attitudes on both sides was to demonstrate the greatest Christian weapon: the love of God. He said, "He that loves not lives not, and he that lives by 'The Life' cannot die." To Muslims he declared, "I come to meet the Muslims not with arms, but with words; not by force, but by reason, not in hate but in love."

(4) Anticipate questions, inquiries, and objections to the unique teaching of the Bible. These must be explained in accordance with the teaching of the Bible. Be patient, ready to answer your Muslim friend's objections as Christ did in His encounter with Nicodemus and the Samaritan woman **(John 3–4)**.

(5) Don't denigrate your Muslim friend's faith. When Christ—the "bright morning star" **(Rev. 22:16)**—radiates, He will eliminate all shadows.

(6) Introduce the life, teaching, and ministry of Christ. (He is highly revered and exalted in Islam). The majority of Muslim converts testify that the most influential factor in their conversion was their exposure to the true words and life of Christ.

(7) Introduce your friend to the Bible. The Word of God is the greatest tool for evangelizing Muslims. We must be encouraged by God's promise: "So shall my word be that goes out from my mouth; it shall not return to me empty, but it shall accomplish that which I purpose, and shall succeed in the thing for which I sent it" **(Isa. 55:11)**. "For the word of God is living and active, sharper than any two-edged sword, piercing to the division of the soul and of spirit, of joints and of marrow, and discerning the thoughts and intentions of the heart" **(Heb. 4:12)**. In introducing your Muslim friends to the Bible, you can focus on two foundational truths about Scripture. First, you can establish the authority of the Bible in order to dispel Muslim objections. Scripture is God's Word. Its source is divine, and its

authority is final and timeless. Second, you can emphasize that the Bible as a whole is one revelation with a singular goal. The overall theme of the Bible is the redemption of sinful man. The Bible is salvation history; it moves progressively, culminating in the coming of Christ. Emphasize that Christ is the central figure in both testaments. From the beginning, God promised the coming of the Messiah, Jesus.

(8) If appropriate, share your personal testimony, and saturate it with the truth of Scripture. Underscore the crucial difference between being a legalistic person and being radically changed by the life, teaching, and power of Christ. Paul's testimony in **Philippians 3** is a profound example of this transformation.

(9) Avoid using theological terms that are foreign to your Muslim friend. But if you must use them, try to clarify their meanings and emphasize their implications for salvation.

(10) Introduce your Muslim friend to your pastor, and invite him to worship with you. Trust The Holy Spirit to bring the lost sheep into the fold.

The Power of the Word of God

A recent example of a Muslim testimony brings out the crucial importance of the power of the Word of God; it often influences a Muslim's decision to embrace the gospel. Hamran was a traditional and devout Muslim leader. While writing a sermon to be delivered in the mosque, he came across the following verse from the Quran: "Say, O people of the Scripture! [Jews and Christians], you will be nothing unless you uphold the Torah and the Gospel, and all that is revealed to you from your Lord" (Surah 5:68). Hamran says:

I have read this verse a hundred times, but at last God whispered to my soul that "Torah" and the "Gospel" which are mentioned in the Quran are the same Torah and the Gospel found in the Bible now. I had always thought that the Torah and the Gospel mentioned in the Quran no longer existed physically, and that their contents had been summarized in the Quran. I was convinced that the Torah and the Gospel, which form the Bible now were false, and that the original contents had been misarranged, forged or added to by people. However, my soul told me that the Torah/Gospel now presented in the Bible is true. My mind constantly opposed this inner voice: "No! The Torah and the Gospel in the Bible have been falsified." My thoughts contradicted my soul and conscience, and I became uncertain and doubtful as to what was right. To make peace with my conscience, I took the problem to God. He helped me recognize the truth of the Gospel as I was reading it.

While God is bringing His lost sheep to Himself, still millions must hear the good news. According to new population projections by the Pew Research Center's Forum on Religion and Public Life, the world Muslim population is expected to increase by about 35 percent in the next twenty years, rising from 1.6 billion in 2010 to 2.2 billion by 2030. As ambassadors for Christ, we ought to face this increase not with fear, but with confidence in the Lord's promises. Jesus said, "I will build my church, and the gates of hell will not prevail against it" **(Matt. 16:18)**. I am certain that the church of Christ eventually will include millions of converted Muslims. God uses people like us to bring them home.

Opportunities for Discipleship through Technology

There was a day that you could disciple people face to face. After the coronavirus, many churches closed their doors, but today, we can use technological means such as satellite broadcast, Instagram, Facebook and internet websites to teach the word of God. In 2016 when the Lord wanted me to share the Gospel using Satellite, I did not know how the Lord was going to use this ministry (Hayate Abadi Ministries) to reach out to Farsi speaking people all around the world. Now, in Iran more people are watching our satellite programs because more are staying at home. They are watching the Gospel message.

Iranians are the number one people in the world most open to the Gospel, and daily, hundreds are saved. Afghanis are number two in the world among people that openly receive the Lord. I preach the Gospel message through Radio broadcasts, and many people in Afghanistan get to hear the word of God through radio.

One day, a man called from Afghanistan and told me his own personal story. He works for someone that allows him to sleep in his shop. One day when the owner left the shop, he listened to my radio broadcast and prayed with me to invite Christ into his heart as his only Lord and Savior. People from every corner of the world are also watching our TV ministry broadcast as I preach the Gospel message and many receive Christ. Accordingly, when people get saved, we start making disciples.

If you are not saved, now is the time for you to repent and invite Jesus Christ into your heart as your only Lord and savior. You can say, "Lord, I am sorry for all of my sins and I truly repent. Jesus, I believe that you are the only son of God that became flesh and died on the cross for my sins. On the third day, you rose again from the dead and you are seated at the right hand of the heavenly Father. I invite you into my heart as my only Lord and Savior. Lord, fill me with your The Holy Spirit so that I can follow you the rest of my life. In Jesus Christ's name I pray."

Know that you can join with the rest of your brothers and sisters in Christ and pray for us. As we share the Gospel, more people will be open to the Gospel. If you are already a disciple, you can help us in this work.

I also strongly recommend that you read the word of God daily and join a biblical church. Do not forget to fellowship with other believers.

I am so thankful to my wife and my sons for being great helpers, and as Joshua said, "As for me and my household we will serve the Lord."

In Christ,
Mark

Please contact me at **mark@hayateabadi.org**.

www.HayateAbadi.org

www.ingramcontent.com/pod-product-compliance
Lightning Source LLC
Chambersburg PA
CBHW021000090426
42736CB00010B/1403